Let Me Tell You About Starting Primary School

by
Katelyn Banks, age 10
with help from Ivy, age 5

For Ivy, the best buddy
I could ever ask for
☺ xxx

Hi, I'm Katelyn and I'm in year 6 at Primary School. That's the top year!

How exciting, you are starting school soon. Shall I tell you about my school so you know what to expect?

At my school, year 6's are paired up with the new children starting reception, to help them settle in. These are called buddies.

This is me and my buddy Ivy.

When you start school, don't worry, you will make lots of friends and the big kids will help look after you.

At school, you get to play lots so you can learn about sharing and being kind.

What do you like to play?

You also get to make things, it's so much fun.

Here is Ivy showing me her Easter egg creation.

When Ivy is learning, she loves to concentrate so she can learn more and more every day.

Me and Ivy love reading together in the library.

Do you like to read?

At lunchtime, you can take a packed lunch or have a school dinner. Both are super yummy!

Me and Ivy always eat together and love telling each other about things we learnt that day. We then go outside to play.

Sometimes we play hide and seek or ring a ring a roses.

You'll do lots of sports and outside games and may have to get changed for these. The teachers will help you.

At sports day, I helped with the games and Ivy won the egg and spoon race.

When you need the toilet just put up your hand. School has special toilets for little people like you. Don't forget to wash your hands!

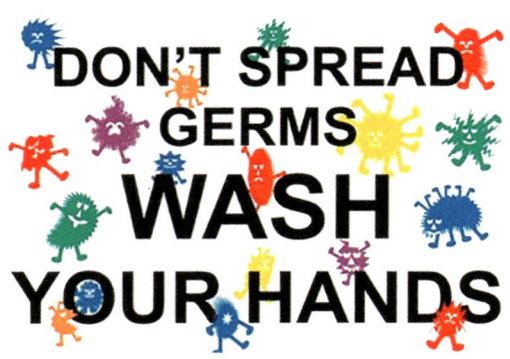

What do you need for Primary School?

Sometimes it's confusing to know what you need for school. I think:

Uniform, School bag, Medication e.g. inhaler, Water bottle, PE kit, Plimsolls, Change of school clothes (in-case of accidents), Wellies, Waterproof Coat, Sun Lotion, Snack each day, Lunch box and lunch (unless Hot Dinners)

When it is time to go home, we give each other one last hug and wave goodbye. We can't wait for the next school day to come!

I have loved being a buddy, have fun and learn lots.

Katelyn xx

About the Author

Katelyn Banks is a ten-year-old girl. She loves reading and writing but is also a keen actress, dancer, singer and guitar player. Katelyn dreams of being a famous actress. She has an amazing sister who she loves loads.

Katelyn lives with her Mum, Dad, Sister and spoilt Chihuahua called Poppy. When Katelyn started school she had a buddy too, called Georgia.

Katelyn (age 5) and her buddy Georgia (age 11), 2013

2019 – age 10 and 17!! – *still friends*

**Ivy and Katelyn
by Ivy**

Printed in Poland
by Amazon Fulfillment
Poland Sp. z o.o., Wrocław

50599913R00016